Child Custody Journal

This Book Belongs To

NAME _____

CONTACT _____

Child Name:		Paying Parcent		Date:	

Payment Information

Date Due	Expected Amount	Actual Amount	Date Paid	Balance

Agreement References

Agreement	Document	Page	Note

Holiday Schedule

Holiday	Time	Even-Numbered Years	Odd-Numbered Years

Visiting Log   S M T W T S F   Date:

Child		Location	
Cutodial Parcent		Non-Custodial Parcent	
Style of Visit			
Expected Start Time		Actual Start Time	
Expected End Time		Actual End Time	

Phone Calls Log

Initiated by		With whom	
Time		Length of call	

Notes: _____

Child Name:		Paying Parcent		Date:	

Payment Information

Date Due	Expected Amount	Actual Amount	Date Paid	Balance

Agreement References

Agreement	Document	Page	Note

Holiday Schedule

Holiday	Time	Even-Numbered Years	Odd-Numbered Years

Visiting Log   S M T W T S F   Date:

Child		Location	
Cutodial Parcent		Non-Custodial Parcent	
Style of Visit			
Expected Start Time		Actual Start Time	
Expected End Time		Actual End Time	

Phone Calls Log

Initiated by		With whom	
Time		Length of call	

Notes: _____

_____

_____

Child Name:		Paying Parcent		Date:	

Payment Information

Date Due	Expected Amount	Actual Amount	Date Paid	Balance

Agreement References

Agreement	Document	Page	Note

Holiday Schedule

Holiday	Time	Even-Numbered Years	Odd-Numbered Years

Visiting Log   S M T W T S F   Date: _____

Child		Location	
Cutodial Parcent		Non-Custodial Parcent	
Style of Visit			
Expected Start Time		Actual Start Time	
Expected End Time		Actual End Time	

Phone Calls Log

Initiated by		With whom	
Time		Length of call	

Notes: _____

_____

_____

| Child Name: | | Paying Parcent | | Date: | |

Payment Information

Date Due	Expected Amount	Actual Amount	Date Paid	Balance

Agreement References

Agreement	Document	Page	Note

Holiday Schedule

Holiday	Time	Even-Numbered Years	Odd-Numbered Years

Visiting Log   [S] [M] [T] [W] [T] [S] [F]   Date:

Child		Location	
Cutodial Parcent		Non-Custodial Parcent	
Style of Visit			
Expected Start Time		Actual Start Time	
Expected End Time		Actual End Time	

Phone Calls Log

Initiated by		With whom	
Time		Length of call	

Notes: _____

_____

_____

| Child Name: | | Paying Parcent | | Date: | |

Payment Information

Date Due	Expected Amount	Actual Amount	Date Paid	Balance

Agreement References

Agreement	Document	Page	Note

Holiday Schedule

Holiday	Time	Even-Numbered Years	Odd-Numbered Years

Visiting Log   S M T W T S F   Date:

Child		Location	
Cutodial Parcent		Non-Custodial Parcent	
Style of Visit			
Expected Start Time		Actual Start Time	
Expected End Time		Actual End Time	

Phone Calls Log

Initiated by		With whom	
Time		Length of call	

Notes: _____

_____

_____

Child Name:		Paying Parcent		Date:	

Payment Information

Date Due	Expected Amount	Actual Amount	Date Paid	Balance

Agreement References

Agreement	Document	Page	Note

Holiday Schedule

Holiday	Time	Even-Numbered Years	Odd-Numbered Years

Visiting Log   S M T W T S F   Date:

Child		Location	
Cutodial Parcent		Non-Custodial Parcent	
Style of Visit			
Expected Start Time		Actual Start Time	
Expected End Time		Actual End Time	

Phone Calls Log

Initiated by		With whom	
Time		Length of call	

Notes: _____
_____

| Child Name: | | Paying Parcent | | Date: | |

Payment Information

Date Due	Expected Amount	Actual Amount	Date Paid	Balance

Agreement References

Agreement	Document	Page	Note

Holiday Schedule

Holiday	Time	Even-Numbered Years	Odd-Numbered Years

Visiting Log S M T W T S F   Date:

Child		Location	
Cutodial Parcent		Non-Custodial Parcent	
Style of Visit			
Expected Start Time		Actual Start Time	
Expected End Time		Actual End Time	

Phone Calls Log

Initiated by		With whom	
Time		Length of call	

Notes: _____

_____

_____

Child Name:		Paying Parent		Date:	

Payment Information

Date Due	Expected Amount	Actual Amount	Date Paid	Balance

Agreement References

Agreement	Document	Page	Note

Holiday Schedule

Holiday	Time	Even-Numbered Years	Odd-Numbered Years

Visiting Log ☐S ☐M ☐T ☐W ☐T ☐S ☐F   Date:

Child		Location	
Cutodial Parcent		Non-Custodial Parcent	
Style of Visit			
Expected Start Time		Actual Start Time	
Expected End Time		Actual End Time	

Phone Calls Log

Initiated by		With whom	
Time		Length of call	

Notes: _____

_____

_____

Child Name:		Paying Parcent		Date:	

Payment Information

Date Due	Expected Amount	Actual Amount	Date Paid	Balance

Agreement References

Agreement	Document	Page	Note

Holiday Schedule

Holiday	Time	Even-Numbered Years	Odd-Numbered Years

Visiting Log   S M T W T S F   Date:

Child		Location	
Cutodial Parcent		Non-Custodial Parcent	
Style of Visit			
Expected Start Time		Actual Start Time	
Expected End Time		Actual End Time	

Phone Calls Log

Initiated by		With whom	
Time		Length of call	

Notes: _____

_____

_____

Child Name:		Paying Parcent		Date:	

Payment Information

Date Due	Expected Amount	Actual Amount	Date Paid	Balance

Agreement References

Agreement	Document	Page	Note

Holiday Schedule

Holiday	Time	Even-Numbered Years	Odd-Numbered Years

Visiting Log   ☐S ☐M ☐T ☐W ☐T ☐S ☐F   Date:

Child		Location	
Cutodial Parcent		Non-Custodial Parcent	
Style of Visit			
Expected Start Time		Actual Start Time	
Expected End Time		Actual End Time	

Phone Calls Log

Initiated by		With whom	
Time		Length of call	

Notes: _____
_____
_____

Child Name:		Paying Parcent		Date:	

Payment Information

Date Due	Expected Amount	Actual Amount	Date Paid	Balance

Agreement References

Agreement	Document	Page	Note

Holiday Schedule

Holiday	Time	Even-Numbered Years	Odd-Numbered Years

Visiting Log   [S] [M] [T] [W] [T] [S] [F]   Date:

Child		Location	
Cutodial Parcent		Non-Custodial Parcent	
Style of Visit			
Expected Start Time		Actual Start Time	
Expected End Time		Actual End Time	

Phone Calls Log

Initiated by		With whom	
Time		Length of call	

Notes: _____

_____

_____

Child Name:		Paying Parent		Date:	

Payment Information

Date Due	Expected Amount	Actual Amount	Date Paid	Balance

Agreement References

Agreement	Document	Page	Note

Holiday Schedule

Holiday	Time	Even-Numbered Years	Odd-Numbered Years

Visiting Log S M T W T S F   Date:

Child		Location	
Cutodial Parcent		Non-Custodial Parcent	
Style of Visit			
Expected Start Time		Actual Start Time	
Expected End Time		Actual End Time	

Phone Calls Log

Initiated by		With whom	
Time		Length of call	

Notes: _____

_____

_____

Child Name:		Paying Parcent		Date:	

Payment Information

Date Due	Expected Amount	Actual Amount	Date Paid	Balance

Agreement References

Agreement	Document	Page	Note

Holiday Schedule

Holiday	Time	Even-Numbered Years	Odd-Numbered Years

Visiting Log S M T W T S F   Date:

Child		Location	
Cutodial Parcent		Non-Custodial Parcent	
Style of Visit			
Expected Start Time		Actual Start Time	
Expected End Time		Actual End Time	

Phone Calls Log

Initiated by		With whom	
Time		Length of call	

Notes: _____

| Child Name: | | Paying Parcent | | Date: | |

Payment Information

Date Due	Expected Amount	Actual Amount	Date Paid	Balance

Agreement References

Agreement	Document	Page	Note

Holiday Schedule

Holiday	Time	Even-Numbered Years	Odd-Numbered Years

Visiting Log   S M T W T S F   Date:

Child		Location	
Cutodial Parcent		Non-Custodial Parcent	
Style of Visit			
Expected Start Time		Actual Start Time	
Expected End Time		Actual End Time	

Phone Calls Log

Initiated by		With whom	
Time		Length of call	

Notes: _____

_____

_____

Child Name:		Paying Parcent		Date:	

Payment Information

Date Due	Expected Amount	Actual Amount	Date Paid	Balance

Agreement References

Agreement	Document	Page	Note

Holiday Schedule

Holiday	Time	Even-Numbered Years	Odd-Numbered Years

Visiting Log   ☐S ☐M ☐T ☐W ☐T ☐S ☐F   Date:

Child		Location	
Cutodial Parcent		Non-Custodial Parcent	
Style of Visit			
Expected Start Time		Actual Start Time	
Expected End Time		Actual End Time	

Phone Calls Log

Initiated by		With whom	
Time		Length of call	

Notes: _____

_____

Child Name:		Paying Parcent		Date:	

Payment Information

Date Due	Expected Amount	Actual Amount	Date Paid	Balance

Agreement References

Agreement	Document	Page	Note

Holiday Schedule

Holiday	Time	Even-Numbered Years	Odd-Numbered Years

Visiting Log S M T W T S F   Date:

Child		Location	
Cutodial Parcent		Non-Custodial Parcent	
Style of Visit			
Expected Start Time		Actual Start Time	
Expected End Time		Actual End Time	

Phone Calls Log

Initiated by		With whom	
Time		Length of call	

Notes: _____

_____

_____

| Child Name: | | Paying Parcent | | Date: | |

Payment Information

Date Due	Expected Amount	Actual Amount	Date Paid	Balance

Agreement References

Agreement	Document	Page	Note

Holiday Schedule

Holiday	Time	Even-Numbered Years	Odd-Numbered Years

Visiting Log   S M T W T S F   Date:

Child		Location	
Cutodial Parcent		Non-Custodial Parcent	
Style of Visit			
Expected Start Time		Actual Start Time	
Expected End Time		Actual End Time	

Phone Calls Log

Initiated by		With whom	
Time		Length of call	

Notes: _____
_____
_____

Child Name:		Paying Parcent		Date:	

Payment Information

Date Due	Expected Amount	Actual Amount	Date Paid	Balance

Agreement References

Agreement	Document	Page	Note

Holiday Schedule

Holiday	Time	Even-Numbered Years	Odd-Numbered Years

Visiting Log   S M T W T S F   Date:

Child		Location	
Cutodial Parcent		Non-Custodial Parcent	
Style of Visit			
Expected Start Time		Actual Start Time	
Expected End Time		Actual End Time	

Phone Calls Log

Initiated by		With whom	
Time		Length of call	

Notes: _____

_____

_____

Child Name:		Paying Parcent		Date:	

Payment Information

Date Due	Expected Amount	Actual Amount	Date Paid	Balance

Agreement References

Agreement	Document	Page	Note

Holiday Schedule

Holiday	Time	Even-Numbered Years	Odd-Numbered Years

Visiting Log   S M T W T S F   Date:

Child		Location	
Cutodial Parcent		Non-Custodial Parcent	
Style of Visit			
Expected Start Time		Actual Start Time	
Expected End Time		Actual End Time	

Phone Calls Log

Initiated by		With whom	
Time		Length of call	

Notes: _____

_____

Child Name:		Paying Parcent		Date:	

Payment Information

Date Due	Expected Amount	Actual Amount	Date Paid	Balance

Agreement References

Agreement	Document	Page	Note

Holiday Schedule

Holiday	Time	Even-Numbered Years	Odd-Numbered Years

Visiting Log   S M T W T S F   Date:

Child		Location	
Cutodial Parcent		Non-Custodial Parcent	
Style of Visit			
Expected Start Time		Actual Start Time	
Expected End Time		Actual End Time	

Phone Calls Log

Initiated by		With whom	
Time		Length of call	

Notes: _____

_____

_____

| Child Name: | | Paying Parcent | | Date: | |

Payment Information

Date Due	Expected Amount	Actual Amount	Date Paid	Balance

Agreement References

Agreement	Document	Page	Note

Holiday Schedule

Holiday	Time	Even-Numbered Years	Odd-Numbered Years

Visiting Log   [S] [M] [T] [W] [T] [S] [F]   Date:

Child		Location	
Cutodial Parcent		Non-Custodial Parcent	
Style of Visit			
Expected Start Time		Actual Start Time	
Expected End Time		Actual End Time	

Phone Calls Log

Initiated by		With whom	
Time		Length of call	

Notes: _____

_____

_____

Child Name:		Paying Parcent		Date:	

Payment Information

Date Due	Expected Amount	Actual Amount	Date Paid	Balance

Agreement References

Agreement	Document	Page	Note

Holiday Schedule

Holiday	Time	Even-Numbered Years	Odd-Numbered Years

Visiting Log S M T W T S F   Date:

Child		Location	
Cutodial Parcent		Non-Custodial Parcent	
Style of Visit			
Expected Start Time		Actual Start Time	
Expected End Time		Actual End Time	

Phone Calls Log

Initiated by		With whom	
Time		Length of call	

Notes: _____

_____

_____

Child Name:		Paying Parcent		Date:	

Payment Information

Date Due	Expected Amount	Actual Amount	Date Paid	Balance

Agreement References

Agreement	Document	Page	Note

Holiday Schedule

Holiday	Time	Even-Numbered Years	Odd-Numbered Years

Visiting Log   S M T W T S F   Date:

Child		Location	
Cutodial Parcent		Non-Custodial Parcent	
Style of Visit			
Expected Start Time		Actual Start Time	
Expected End Time		Actual End Time	

Phone Calls Log

Initiated by		With whom	
Time		Length of call	

Notes: _____

Child Name:		Paying Parcent		Date:	

Payment Information

Date Due	Expected Amount	Actual Amount	Date Paid	Balance

Agreement References

Agreement	Document	Page	Note

Holiday Schedule

Holiday	Time	Even-Numbered Years	Odd-Numbered Years

Visiting Log   S M T W T S F   Date:

Child		Location	
Cutodial Parcent		Non-Custodial Parcent	
Style of Visit			
Expected Start Time		Actual Start Time	
Expected End Time		Actual End Time	

Phone Calls Log

Initiated by		With whom	
Time		Length of call	

Notes: _____

_____

_____

Child Name:		Paying Parcent		Date:	

Payment Information

Date Due	Expected Amount	Actual Amount	Date Paid	Balance

Agreement References

Agreement	Document	Page	Note

Holiday Schedule

Holiday	Time	Even-Numbered Years	Odd-Numbered Years

Visiting Log   S M T W T S F   Date:

Child		Location	
Cutodial Parcent		Non-Custodial Parcent	
Style of Visit			
Expected Start Time		Actual Start Time	
Expected End Time		Actual End Time	

Phone Calls Log

Initiated by		With whom	
Time		Length of call	

Notes: _____

_____

Child Name:		Paying Parcent		Date:	

Payment Information

Date Due	Expected Amount	Actual Amount	Date Paid	Balance

Agreement References

Agreement	Document	Page	Note

Holiday Schedule

Holiday	Time	Even-Numbered Years	Odd-Numbered Years

Visiting Log   ☐S ☐M ☐T ☐W ☐T ☐S ☐F   Date:

Child		Location	
Cutodial Parcent		Non-Custodial Parcent	
Style of Visit			
Expected Start Time		Actual Start Time	
Expected End Time		Actual End Time	

Phone Calls Log

Initiated by		With whom	
Time		Length of call	

Notes: _____

_____

_____

Child Name:			Paying Parcent		Date:	

Payment Information

Date Due	Expected Amount	Actual Amount	Date Paid	Balance

Agreement References

Agreement	Document	Page	Note

Holiday Schedule

Holiday	Time	Even-Numbered Years	Odd-Numbered Years

Visiting Log   S M T W T S F   Date:

Child		Location	
Cutodial Parcent		Non-Custodial Parcent	
Style of Visit			
Expected Start Time		Actual Start Time	
Expected End Time		Actual End Time	

Phone Calls Log

Initiated by		With whom	
Time		Length of call	

Notes: _____

_____

Child Name:		Paying Parcent		Date:	

Payment Information

Date Due	Expected Amount	Actual Amount	Date Paid	Balance

Agreement References

Agreement	Document	Page	Note

Holiday Schedule

Holiday	Time	Even-Numbered Years	Odd-Numbered Years

Visiting Log   ☐S ☐M ☐T ☐W ☐T ☐S ☐F   Date:

Child		Location	
Cutodial Parcent		Non-Custodial Parcent	
Style of Visit			
Expected Start Time		Actual Start Time	
Expected End Time		Actual End Time	

Phone Calls Log

Initiated by		With whom	
Time		Length of call	

Notes: _____

_____

_____

Child Name:		Paying Parcent		Date:	

Payment Information

Date Due	Expected Amount	Actual Amount	Date Paid	Balance

Agreement References

Agreement	Document	Page	Note

Holiday Schedule

Holiday	Time	Even-Numbered Years	Odd-Numbered Years

Visiting Log   S M T W T S F   Date:

Child		Location	
Cutodial Parcent		Non-Custodial Parcent	
Style of Visit			
Expected Start Time		Actual Start Time	
Expected End Time		Actual End Time	

Phone Calls Log

Initiated by		With whom	
Time		Length of call	

Notes: _____

_____

_____

Child Name:		Paying Parcent		Date:	

Payment Information

Date Due	Expected Amount	Actual Amount	Date Paid	Balance

Agreement References

Agreement	Document	Page	Note

Holiday Schedule

Holiday	Time	Even-Numbered Years	Odd-Numbered Years

Visiting Log   S M T W T S F   Date:

Child		Location	
Cutodial Parcent		Non-Custodial Parcent	
Style of Visit			
Expected Start Time		Actual Start Time	
Expected End Time		Actual End Time	

Phone Calls Log

Initiated by		With whom	
Time		Length of call	

Notes: _____

_____

_____

Child Name:		Paying Parcent		Date:	

Payment Information

Date Due	Expected Amount	Actual Amount	Date Paid	Balance

Agreement References

Agreement	Document	Page	Note

Holiday Schedule

Holiday	Time	Even-Numbered Years	Odd-Numbered Years

Visiting Log   [S] [M] [T] [W] [T] [S] [F]   Date:

Child		Location	
Cutodial Parcent		Non-Custodial Parcent	
Style of Visit			
Expected Start Time		Actual Start Time	
Expected End Time		Actual End Time	

Phone Calls Log

Initiated by		With whom	
Time		Length of call	

Notes: _____

Child Name:		Paying Parcent		Date:	

Payment Information

Date Due	Expected Amount	Actual Amount	Date Paid	Balance

Agreement References

Agreement	Document	Page	Note

Holiday Schedule

Holiday	Time	Even-Numbered Years	Odd-Numbered Years

Visiting Log   S M T W T S F   Date:

Child		Location	
Cutodial Parcent		Non-Custodial Parcent	
Style of Visit			
Expected Start Time		Actual Start Time	
Expected End Time		Actual End Time	

Phone Calls Log

Initiated by		With whom	
Time		Length of call	

Notes: _____

_____

_____

Child Name:		Paying Parcent		Date:	

Payment Information

Date Due	Expected Amount	Actual Amount	Date Paid	Balance

Agreement References

Agreement	Document	Page	Note

Holiday Schedule

Holiday	Time	Even-Numbered Years	Odd-Numbered Years

Visiting Log ☐S ☐M ☐T ☐W ☐T ☐S ☐F   Date:

Child		Location	
Cutodial Parcent		Non-Custodial Parcent	
Style of Visit			
Expected Start Time		Actual Start Time	
Expected End Time		Actual End Time	

Phone Calls Log

Initiated by		With whom	
Time		Length of call	

Notes: _____

Child Name:		Paying Parcent		Date:	

Payment Information

Date Due	Expected Amount	Actual Amount	Date Paid	Balance

Agreement References

Agreement	Document	Page	Note

Holiday Schedule

Holiday	Time	Even-Numbered Years	Odd-Numbered Years

Visiting Log   ☐S ☐M ☐T ☐W ☐T ☐S ☐F   Date:

Child		Location	
Cutodial Parcent		Non-Custodial Parcent	
Style of Visit			
Expected Start Time		Actual Start Time	
Expected End Time		Actual End Time	

Phone Calls Log

Initiated by		With whom	
Time		Length of call	

Notes: _____
_____

Child Name:		Paying Parcent		Date:	

Payment Information

Date Due	Expected Amount	Actual Amount	Date Paid	Balance

Agreement References

Agreement	Document	Page	Note

Holiday Schedule

Holiday	Time	Even-Numbered Years	Odd-Numbered Years

Visiting Log   S M T W T S F   Date:

Child		Location	
Cutodial Parcent		Non-Custodial Parcent	
Style of Visit			
Expected Start Time		Actual Start Time	
Expected End Time		Actual End Time	

Phone Calls Log

Initiated by		With whom	
Time		Length of call	

Notes: _____

_____

_____

| Child Name: | | Paying Parcent | | Date: | |

Payment Information

Date Due	Expected Amount	Actual Amount	Date Paid	Balance

Agreement References

Agreement	Document	Page	Note

Holiday Schedule

Holiday	Time	Even-Numbered Years	Odd-Numbered Years

Visiting Log S M T W T S F   Date:

Child		Location	
Cutodial Parcent		Non-Custodial Parcent	
Style of Visit			
Expected Start Time		Actual Start Time	
Expected End Time		Actual End Time	

Phone Calls Log

Initiated by		With whom	
Time		Length of call	

Notes: _____

_____

_____

Child Name:		Paying Parcent		Date:	

Payment Information

Date Due	Expected Amount	Actual Amount	Date Paid	Balance

Agreement References

Agreement	Document	Page	Note

Holiday Schedule

Holiday	Time	Even-Numbered Years	Odd-Numbered Years

Visiting Log   S M T W T S F   Date:

Child		Location	
Cutodial Parcent		Non-Custodial Parcent	
Style of Visit			
Expected Start Time		Actual Start Time	
Expected End Time		Actual End Time	

Phone Calls Log

Initiated by		With whom	
Time		Length of call	

Notes: _____

_____

_____

Child Name:		Paying Parcent		Date:	

Payment Information

Date Due	Expected Amount	Actual Amount	Date Paid	Balance

Agreement References

Agreement	Document	Page	Note

Holiday Schedule

Holiday	Time	Even-Numbered Years	Odd-Numbered Years

Visiting Log   S M T W T S F   Date:

Child		Location	
Cutodial Parcent		Non-Custodial Parcent	
Style of Visit			
Expected Start Time		Actual Start Time	
Expected End Time		Actual End Time	

Phone Calls Log

Initiated by		With whom	
Time		Length of call	

Notes: _____
_____
_____

| Child Name: | | Paying Parcent | | Date: | |

Payment Information

Date Due	Expected Amount	Actual Amount	Date Paid	Balance

Agreement References

Agreement	Document	Page	Note

Holiday Schedule

Holiday	Time	Even-Numbered Years	Odd-Numbered Years

Visiting Log   S M T W T S F   Date:

Child		Location	
Cutodial Parcent		Non-Custodial Parcent	
Style of Visit			
Expected Start Time		Actual Start Time	
Expected End Time		Actual End Time	

Phone Calls Log

Initiated by		With whom	
Time		Length of call	

Notes: _____

Child Name:		Paying Parcent		Date:	

Payment Information

Date Due	Expected Amount	Actual Amount	Date Paid	Balance

Agreement References

Agreement	Document	Page	Note

Holiday Schedule

Holiday	Time	Even-Numbered Years	Odd-Numbered Years

Visiting Log   S M T W T S F   Date:

Child		Location	
Cutodial Parcent		Non-Custodial Parcent	
Style of Visit			
Expected Start Time		Actual Start Time	
Expected End Time		Actual End Time	

Phone Calls Log

Initiated by		With whom	
Time		Length of call	

Notes: _____

Child Name:		Paying Parcent		Date:	

Payment Information

Date Due	Expected Amount	Actual Amount	Date Paid	Balance

Agreement References

Agreement	Document	Page	Note

Holiday Schedule

Holiday	Time	Even-Numbered Years	Odd-Numbered Years

Visiting Log [S] [M] [T] [W] [T] [S] [F]   Date:

Child		Location	
Cutodial Parcent		Non-Custodial Parcent	
Style of Visit			
Expected Start Time		Actual Start Time	
Expected End Time		Actual End Time	

Phone Calls Log

Initiated by		With whom	
Time		Length of call	

Notes: _____

_____

Child Name:		Paying Parcent		Date:	

Payment Information

Date Due	Expected Amount	Actual Amount	Date Paid	Balance

Agreement References

Agreement	Document	Page	Note

Holiday Schedule

Holiday	Time	Even-Numbered Years	Odd-Numbered Years

Visiting Log S M T W T S F   Date:

Child		Location	
Cutodial Parcent		Non-Custodial Parcent	
Style of Visit			
Expected Start Time		Actual Start Time	
Expected End Time		Actual End Time	

Phone Calls Log

Initiated by		With whom	
Time		Length of call	

Notes: _____

_____

Child Name:		Paying Parcent		Date:	

Payment Information

Date Due	Expected Amount	Actual Amount	Date Paid	Balance

Agreement References

Agreement	Document	Page	Note

Holiday Schedule

Holiday	Time	Even-Numbered Years	Odd-Numbered Years

Visiting Log   ☐S ☐M ☐T ☐W ☐T ☐S ☐F   Date:

Child		Location	
Cutodial Parcent		Non-Custodial Parcent	
Style of Visit			
Expected Start Time		Actual Start Time	
Expected End Time		Actual End Time	

Phone Calls Log

Initiated by		With whom	
Time		Length of call	

Notes: _____

Child Name:			Paying Parcent		Date:	

Payment Information

Date Due	Expected Amount	Actual Amount	Date Paid	Balance

Agreement References

Agreement	Document	Page	Note

Holiday Schedule

Holiday	Time	Even-Numbered Years	Odd-Numbered Years

Visiting Log   S M T W T S F   Date:

Child		Location	
Cutodial Parcent		Non-Custodial Parcent	
Style of Visit			
Expected Start Time		Actual Start Time	
Expected End Time		Actual End Time	

Phone Calls Log

Initiated by		With whom	
Time		Length of call	

Notes: _____

_____

_____

Child Name:		Paying Parcent		Date:	

Payment Information

Date Due	Expected Amount	Actual Amount	Date Paid	Balance

Agreement References

Agreement	Document	Page	Note

Holiday Schedule

Holiday	Time	Even-Numbered Years	Odd-Numbered Years

Visiting Log   [S] [M] [T] [W] [T] [S] [F]   Date:

Child		Location	
Cutodial Parcent		Non-Custodial Parcent	
Style of Visit			
Expected Start Time		Actual Start Time	
Expected End Time		Actual End Time	

Phone Calls Log

Initiated by		With whom	
Time		Length of call	

Notes: _____

| Child Name: | | Paying Parcent | | Date: | |

Payment Information

Date Due	Expected Amount	Actual Amount	Date Paid	Balance

Agreement References

Agreement	Document	Page	Note

Holiday Schedule

Holiday	Time	Even-Numbered Years	Odd-Numbered Years

Visiting Log S M T W T S F   Date:

Child		Location	
Cutodial Parcent		Non-Custodial Parcent	
Style of Visit			
Expected Start Time		Actual Start Time	
Expected End Time		Actual End Time	

Phone Calls Log

Initiated by		With whom	
Time		Length of call	

Notes: _____

_____

_____

| Child Name: | | Paying Parcent | | Date: | |

Payment Information

Date Due	Expected Amount	Actual Amount	Date Paid	Balance

Agreement References

Agreement	Document	Page	Note

Holiday Schedule

Holiday	Time	Even-Numbered Years	Odd-Numbered Years

Visiting Log   S M T W T S F   Date:

Child		Location	
Cutodial Parcent		Non-Custodial Parcent	
Style of Visit			
Expected Start Time		Actual Start Time	
Expected End Time		Actual End Time	

Phone Calls Log

Initiated by		With whom	
Time		Length of call	

Notes: _____

Child Name:		Paying Parcent		Date:	

Payment Information

Date Due	Expected Amount	Actual Amount	Date Paid	Balance

Agreement References

Agreement	Document	Page	Note

Holiday Schedule

Holiday	Time	Even-Numbered Years	Odd-Numbered Years

Visiting Log   S M T W T S F   Date:

Child		Location	
Cutodial Parcent		Non-Custodial Parcent	
Style of Visit			
Expected Start Time		Actual Start Time	
Expected End Time		Actual End Time	

Phone Calls Log

Initiated by		With whom	
Time		Length of call	

Notes: _____

_____

_____

| Child Name: | | Paying Parcent | | Date: | |

Payment Information

Date Due	Expected Amount	Actual Amount	Date Paid	Balance

Agreement References

Agreement	Document	Page	Note

Holiday Schedule

Holiday	Time	Even-Numbered Years	Odd-Numbered Years

Visiting Log   S M T W T S F   Date:

Child		Location	
Cutodial Parcent		Non-Custodial Parcent	
Style of Visit			
Expected Start Time		Actual Start Time	
Expected End Time		Actual End Time	

Phone Calls Log

Initiated by		With whom	
Time		Length of call	

Notes: _____

| Child Name: | | Paying Parcent | | Date: | |

Payment Information

Date Due	Expected Amount	Actual Amount	Date Paid	Balance

Agreement References

Agreement	Document	Page	Note

Holiday Schedule

Holiday	Time	Even-Numbered Years	Odd-Numbered Years

Visiting Log   S M T W T S F   Date:

Child		Location	
Cutodial Parcent		Non-Custodial Parcent	
Style of Visit			
Expected Start Time		Actual Start Time	
Expected End Time		Actual End Time	

Phone Calls Log

Initiated by		With whom	
Time		Length of call	

Notes: _____

_____

_____

Child Name:		Paying Parcent		Date:	

Payment Information

Date Due	Expected Amount	Actual Amount	Date Paid	Balance

Agreement References

Agreement	Document	Page	Note

Holiday Schedule

Holiday	Time	Even-Numbered Years	Odd-Numbered Years

Visiting Log   S M T W T S F   Date:

Child		Location	
Cutodial Parcent		Non-Custodial Parcent	
Style of Visit			
Expected Start Time		Actual Start Time	
Expected End Time		Actual End Time	

Phone Calls Log

Initiated by		With whom	
Time		Length of call	

Notes: _____

Child Name:		Paying Parcent		Date:	

Payment Information

Date Due	Expected Amount	Actual Amount	Date Paid	Balance

Agreement References

Agreement	Document	Page	Note

Holiday Schedule

Holiday	Time	Even-Numbered Years	Odd-Numbered Years

Visiting Log   S M T W T S F   Date: _____

Child		Location	
Cutodial Parcent		Non-Custodial Parcent	
Style of Visit			
Expected Start Time		Actual Start Time	
Expected End Time		Actual End Time	

Phone Calls Log

Initiated by		With whom	
Time		Length of call	

Notes: _____

_____

_____

Child Name:			Paying Parcent		Date:	

Payment Information

Date Due	Expected Amount	Actual Amount	Date Paid	Balance

Agreement References

Agreement	Document	Page	Note

Holiday Schedule

Holiday	Time	Even-Numbered Years	Odd-Numbered Years

Visiting Log   S M T W T S F   Date:

Child		Location	
Cutodial Parcent		Non-Custodial Parcent	
Style of Visit			
Expected Start Time		Actual Start Time	
Expected End Time		Actual End Time	

Phone Calls Log

Initiated by		With whom	
Time		Length of call	

Notes: _____

Child Name:		Paying Parcent		Date:	

Payment Information

Date Due	Expected Amount	Actual Amount	Date Paid	Balance

Agreement References

Agreement	Document	Page	Note

Holiday Schedule

Holiday	Time	Even-Numbered Years	Odd-Numbered Years

Visiting Log S M T W T S F   Date:

Child		Location	
Cutodial Parcent		Non-Custodial Parcent	
Style of Visit			
Expected Start Time		Actual Start Time	
Expected End Time		Actual End Time	

Phone Calls Log

Initiated by		With whom	
Time		Length of call	

Notes: _____

_____

| Child Name: | | Paying Parcent | | Date: | |

Payment Information

Date Due	Expected Amount	Actual Amount	Date Paid	Balance

Agreement References

Agreement	Document	Page	Note

Holiday Schedule

Holiday	Time	Even-Numbered Years	Odd-Numbered Years

Visiting Log ☐S ☐M ☐T ☐W ☐T ☐S ☐F   Date:

Child		Location	
Cutodial Parcent		Non-Custodial Parcent	
Style of Visit			
Expected Start Time		Actual Start Time	
Expected End Time		Actual End Time	

Phone Calls Log

Initiated by		With whom	
Time		Length of call	

Notes: _____

| Child Name: | | Paying Parcent | | Date: | |

Payment Information

Date Due	Expected Amount	Actual Amount	Date Paid	Balance

Agreement References

Agreement	Document	Page	Note

Holiday Schedule

Holiday	Time	Even-Numbered Years	Odd-Numbered Years

Visiting Log

☐ S ☐ M ☐ T ☐ W ☐ T ☐ S ☐ F   Date:

Child		Location	
Cutodial Parcent		Non-Custodial Parcent	
Style of Visit			
Expected Start Time		Actual Start Time	
Expected End Time		Actual End Time	

Phone Calls Log

Initiated by		With whom	
Time		Length of call	

Notes: _____

_____

_____

Child Name:		Paying Parcent		Date:	

Payment Information

Date Due	Expected Amount	Actual Amount	Date Paid	Balance

Agreement References

Agreement	Document	Page	Note

Holiday Schedule

Holiday	Time	Even-Numbered Years	Odd-Numbered Years

Visiting Log   [S] [M] [T] [W] [T] [S] [F]   Date:

Child		Location	
Cutodial Parcent		Non-Custodial Parcent	
Style of Visit			
Expected Start Time		Actual Start Time	
Expected End Time		Actual End Time	

Phone Calls Log

Initiated by		With whom	
Time		Length of call	

Notes: _____

_____

Child Name:		Paying Parcent		Date:	

Payment Information

Date Due	Expected Amount	Actual Amount	Date Paid	Balance

Agreement References

Agreement	Document	Page	Note

Holiday Schedule

Holiday	Time	Even-Numbered Years	Odd-Numbered Years

Visiting Log   S M T W T S F   Date:

Child		Location	
Cutodial Parcent		Non-Custodial Parcent	
Style of Visit			
Expected Start Time		Actual Start Time	
Expected End Time		Actual End Time	

Phone Calls Log

Initiated by		With whom	
Time		Length of call	

Notes: _____

_____

_____

Child Name:		Paying Parcent		Date:	

Payment Information

Date Due	Expected Amount	Actual Amount	Date Paid	Balance

Agreement References

Agreement	Document	Page	Note

Holiday Schedule

Holiday	Time	Even-Numbered Years	Odd-Numbered Years

Visiting Log S M T W T S F   Date:

Child		Location	
Cutodial Parcent		Non-Custodial Parcent	
Style of Visit			
Expected Start Time		Actual Start Time	
Expected End Time		Actual End Time	

Phone Calls Log

Initiated by		With whom	
Time		Length of call	

Notes: _____

Child Name:		Paying Parcent		Date:	

Payment Information

Date Due	Expected Amount	Actual Amount	Date Paid	Balance

Agreement References

Agreement	Document	Page	Note

Holiday Schedule

Holiday	Time	Even-Numbered Years	Odd-Numbered Years

Visiting Log [S] [M] [T] [W] [T] [S] [F]   Date:

Child		Location	
Cutodial Parcent		Non-Custodial Parcent	
Style of Visit			
Expected Start Time		Actual Start Time	
Expected End Time		Actual End Time	

Phone Calls Log

Initiated by		With whom	
Time		Length of call	

Notes: _____

_____

_____

| Child Name: | | Paying Parcent | | Date: | |

Payment Information

Date Due	Expected Amount	Actual Amount	Date Paid	Balance

Agreement References

Agreement	Document	Page	Note

Holiday Schedule

Holiday	Time	Even-Numbered Years	Odd-Numbered Years

Visiting Log   S M T W T S F   Date:

Child		Location	
Cutodial Parcent		Non-Custodial Parcent	
Style of Visit			
Expected Start Time		Actual Start Time	
Expected End Time		Actual End Time	

Phone Calls Log

Initiated by		With whom	
Time		Length of call	

Notes: _____

Child Name:		Paying Parcent		Date:	

Payment Information

Date Due	Expected Amount	Actual Amount	Date Paid	Balance

Agreement References

Agreement	Document	Page	Note

Holiday Schedule

Holiday	Time	Even-Numbered Years	Odd-Numbered Years

Visiting Log ☐S ☐M ☐T ☐W ☐T ☐S ☐F   Date:

Child		Location	
Cutodial Parcent		Non-Custodial Parcent	
Style of Visit			
Expected Start Time		Actual Start Time	
Expected End Time		Actual End Time	

Phone Calls Log

Initiated by		With whom	
Time		Length of call	

Notes: _____
_____

Child Name:		Paying Parcent		Date:	

Payment Information

Date Due	Expected Amount	Actual Amount	Date Paid	Balance

Agreement References

Agreement	Document	Page	Note

Holiday Schedule

Holiday	Time	Even-Numbered Years	Odd-Numbered Years

Visiting Log   S M T W T S F   Date:

Child		Location	
Cutodial Parcent		Non-Custodial Parcent	
Style of Visit			
Expected Start Time		Actual Start Time	
Expected End Time		Actual End Time	

Phone Calls Log

Initiated by		With whom	
Time		Length of call	

Notes: _____

_____

_____

Child Name:		Paying Parent		Date:	

Payment Information

Date Due	Expected Amount	Actual Amount	Date Paid	Balance

Agreement References

Agreement	Document	Page	Note

Holiday Schedule

Holiday	Time	Even-Numbered Years	Odd-Numbered Years

Visiting Log   S M T W T S F   Date:

Child		Location	
Cutodial Parcent		Non-Custodial Parcent	
Style of Visit			
Expected Start Time		Actual Start Time	
Expected End Time		Actual End Time	

Phone Calls Log

Initiated by		With whom	
Time		Length of call	

Notes: _____

_____

_____

| Child Name: | | Paying Parcent | | Date: | |

Payment Information

Date Due	Expected Amount	Actual Amount	Date Paid	Balance

Agreement References

Agreement	Document	Page	Note

Holiday Schedule

Holiday	Time	Even-Numbered Years	Odd-Numbered Years

Visiting Log   S M T W T S F   Date:

Child		Location	
Cutodial Parcent		Non-Custodial Parcent	
Style of Visit			
Expected Start Time		Actual Start Time	
Expected End Time		Actual End Time	

Phone Calls Log

Initiated by		With whom	
Time		Length of call	

Notes: _____

Child Name:		Paying Parcent		Date:	

Payment Information

Date Due	Expected Amount	Actual Amount	Date Paid	Balance

Agreement References

Agreement	Document	Page	Note

Holiday Schedule

Holiday	Time	Even-Numbered Years	Odd-Numbered Years

Visiting Log   S M T W T S F   Date:

Child		Location	
Cutodial Parcent		Non-Custodial Parcent	
Style of Visit			
Expected Start Time		Actual Start Time	
Expected End Time		Actual End Time	

Phone Calls Log

Initiated by		With whom	
Time		Length of call	

Notes: _____

_____

_____

| Child Name: | | Paying Parcent | | Date: | |

Payment Information

Date Due	Expected Amount	Actual Amount	Date Paid	Balance

Agreement References

Agreement	Document	Page	Note

Holiday Schedule

Holiday	Time	Even-Numbered Years	Odd-Numbered Years

Visiting Log   S M T W T S F   Date:

Child		Location	
Cutodial Parcent		Non-Custodial Parcent	
Style of Visit			
Expected Start Time		Actual Start Time	
Expected End Time		Actual End Time	

Phone Calls Log

Initiated by		With whom	
Time		Length of call	

Notes: _____

Child Name:		Paying Parcent		Date:	

Payment Information

Date Due	Expected Amount	Actual Amount	Date Paid	Balance

Agreement References

Agreement	Document	Page	Note

Holiday Schedule

Holiday	Time	Even-Numbered Years	Odd-Numbered Years

Visiting Log [S] [M] [T] [W] [T] [S] [F]   Date:

Child		Location	
Cutodial Parcent		Non-Custodial Parcent	
Style of Visit			
Expected Start Time		Actual Start Time	
Expected End Time		Actual End Time	

Phone Calls Log

Initiated by		With whom	
Time		Length of call	

Notes: _____

_____

_____

Child Name:		Paying Parent		Date:	

Payment Information

Date Due	Expected Amount	Actual Amount	Date Paid	Balance

Agreement References

Agreement	Document	Page	Note

Holiday Schedule

Holiday	Time	Even-Numbered Years	Odd-Numbered Years

Visiting Log   S M T W T S F   Date:

Child		Location	
Cutodial Parcent		Non-Custodial Parcent	
Style of Visit			
Expected Start Time		Actual Start Time	
Expected End Time		Actual End Time	

Phone Calls Log

Initiated by		With whom	
Time		Length of call	

Notes: _____

_____

Child Name:		Paying Parcent		Date:	

Payment Information

Date Due	Expected Amount	Actual Amount	Date Paid	Balance

Agreement References

Agreement	Document	Page	Note

Holiday Schedule

Holiday	Time	Even-Numbered Years	Odd-Numbered Years

Visiting Log   S M T W T S F   Date:

Child		Location	
Cutodial Parcent		Non-Custodial Parcent	
Style of Visit			
Expected Start Time		Actual Start Time	
Expected End Time		Actual End Time	

Phone Calls Log

Initiated by		With whom	
Time		Length of call	

Notes: _____

_____

Child Name:		Paying Parcent		Date:	

Payment Information

Date Due	Expected Amount	Actual Amount	Date Paid	Balance

Agreement References

Agreement	Document	Page	Note

Holiday Schedule

Holiday	Time	Even-Numbered Years	Odd-Numbered Years

Visiting Log   ☐S ☐M ☐T ☐W ☐T ☐S ☐F   Date:

Child		Location	
Cutodial Parcent		Non-Custodial Parcent	
Style of Visit			
Expected Start Time		Actual Start Time	
Expected End Time		Actual End Time	

Phone Calls Log

Initiated by		With whom	
Time		Length of call	

Notes: _____

_____

Child Name:		Paying Parcent		Date:	

Payment Information

Date Due	Expected Amount	Actual Amount	Date Paid	Balance

Agreement References

Agreement	Document	Page	Note

Holiday Schedule

Holiday	Time	Even-Numbered Years	Odd-Numbered Years

Visiting Log   S M T W T S F   Date:

Child		Location	
Cutodial Parcent		Non-Custodial Parcent	
Style of Visit			
Expected Start Time		Actual Start Time	
Expected End Time		Actual End Time	

Phone Calls Log

Initiated by		With whom	
Time		Length of call	

Notes: _____

_____

_____

| Child Name: | | Paying Parcent | | Date: | |

Payment Information

Date Due	Expected Amount	Actual Amount	Date Paid	Balance

Agreement References

Agreement	Document	Page	Note

Holiday Schedule

Holiday	Time	Even-Numbered Years	Odd-Numbered Years

Visiting Log   S M T W T S F   Date:

Child		Location	
Cutodial Parcent		Non-Custodial Parcent	
Style of Visit			
Expected Start Time		Actual Start Time	
Expected End Time		Actual End Time	

Phone Calls Log

Initiated by		With whom	
Time		Length of call	

Notes: _____

Child Name:			Paying Parcent		Date:	

Payment Information

Date Due	Expected Amount	Actual Amount	Date Paid	Balance

Agreement References

Agreement	Document	Page	Note

Holiday Schedule

Holiday	Time	Even-Numbered Years	Odd-Numbered Years

Visiting Log   S M T W T S F   Date:

Child		Location	
Cutodial Parcent		Non-Custodial Parcent	
Style of Visit			
Expected Start Time		Actual Start Time	
Expected End Time		Actual End Time	

Phone Calls Log

Initiated by		With whom	
Time		Length of call	

Notes: _____
_____
_____

| Child Name: | | Paying Parcent | | Date: | |

Payment Information

Date Due	Expected Amount	Actual Amount	Date Paid	Balance

Agreement References

Agreement	Document	Page	Note

Holiday Schedule

Holiday	Time	Even-Numbered Years	Odd-Numbered Years

Visiting Log   S M T W T S F   Date:

Child		Location	
Cutodial Parcent		Non-Custodial Parcent	
Style of Visit			
Expected Start Time		Actual Start Time	
Expected End Time		Actual End Time	

Phone Calls Log

Initiated by		With whom	
Time		Length of call	

Notes: _____

Child Name:			Paying Parcent		Date:	

Payment Information

Date Due	Expected Amount	Actual Amount	Date Paid	Balance

Agreement References

Agreement	Document	Page	Note

Holiday Schedule

Holiday	Time	Even-Numbered Years	Odd-Numbered Years

Visiting Log   [S] [M] [T] [W] [T] [S] [F]   Date:

Child		Location	
Cutodial Parcent		Non-Custodial Parcent	
Style of Visit			
Expected Start Time		Actual Start Time	
Expected End Time		Actual End Time	

Phone Calls Log

Initiated by		With whom	
Time		Length of call	

Notes: _____

| Child Name: | | Paying Parcent | | Date: | |

Payment Information

Date Due	Expected Amount	Actual Amount	Date Paid	Balance

Agreement References

Agreement	Document	Page	Note

Holiday Schedule

Holiday	Time	Even-Numbered Years	Odd-Numbered Years

Visiting Log ☐S ☐M ☐T ☐W ☐T ☐S ☐F   Date:

Child		Location	
Cutodial Parcent		Non-Custodial Parcent	
Style of Visit			
Expected Start Time		Actual Start Time	
Expected End Time		Actual End Time	

Phone Calls Log

Initiated by		With whom	
Time		Length of call	

Notes: _____

_____

_____

Child Name:		Paying Parcent		Date:	

Payment Information

Date Due	Expected Amount	Actual Amount	Date Paid	Balance

Agreement References

Agreement	Document	Page	Note

Holiday Schedule

Holiday	Time	Even-Numbered Years	Odd-Numbered Years

Visiting Log   S M T W T S F   Date:

Child		Location	
Cutodial Parcent		Non-Custodial Parcent	
Style of Visit			
Expected Start Time		Actual Start Time	
Expected End Time		Actual End Time	

Phone Calls Log

Initiated by		With whom	
Time		Length of call	

Notes: _____

_____

_____

Child Name:		Paying Parcent		Date:	

Payment Information

Date Due	Expected Amount	Actual Amount	Date Paid	Balance

Agreement References

Agreement	Document	Page	Note

Holiday Schedule

Holiday	Time	Even-Numbered Years	Odd-Numbered Years

Visiting Log   [S] [M] [T] [W] [T] [S] [F]   Date:

Child		Location	
Cutodial Parcent		Non-Custodial Parcent	
Style of Visit			
Expected Start Time		Actual Start Time	
Expected End Time		Actual End Time	

Phone Calls Log

Initiated by		With whom	
Time		Length of call	

Notes: _____

Child Name:		Paying Parcent		Date:	

Payment Information

Date Due	Expected Amount	Actual Amount	Date Paid	Balance

Agreement References

Agreement	Document	Page	Note

Holiday Schedule

Holiday	Time	Even-Numbered Years	Odd-Numbered Years

Visiting Log   S M T W T S F   Date:

Child		Location	
Cutodial Parcent		Non-Custodial Parcent	
Style of Visit			
Expected Start Time		Actual Start Time	
Expected End Time		Actual End Time	

Phone Calls Log

Initiated by		With whom	
Time		Length of call	

Notes: _____

_____

_____

Child Name:		Paying Parcent		Date:	

Payment Information

Date Due	Expected Amount	Actual Amount	Date Paid	Balance

Agreement References

Agreement	Document	Page	Note

Holiday Schedule

Holiday	Time	Even-Numbered Years	Odd-Numbered Years

Visiting Log S M T W T S F   Date:

Child		Location	
Cutodial Parcent		Non-Custodial Parcent	
Style of Visit			
Expected Start Time		Actual Start Time	
Expected End Time		Actual End Time	

Phone Calls Log

Initiated by		With whom	
Time		Length of call	

Notes: _____

Child Name:		Paying Parcent		Date:	

Payment Information

Date Due	Expected Amount	Actual Amount	Date Paid	Balance

Agreement References

Agreement	Document	Page	Note

Holiday Schedule

Holiday	Time	Even-Numbered Years	Odd-Numbered Years

Visiting Log   S M T W T S F   Date:

Child		Location	
Cutodial Parcent		Non-Custodial Parcent	
Style of Visit			
Expected Start Time		Actual Start Time	
Expected End Time		Actual End Time	

Phone Calls Log

Initiated by		With whom	
Time		Length of call	

Notes: _____

_____

_____

| Child Name: | | Paying Parcent | | Date: | |

Payment Information

Date Due	Expected Amount	Actual Amount	Date Paid	Balance

Agreement References

Agreement	Document	Page	Note

Holiday Schedule

Holiday	Time	Even-Numbered Years	Odd-Numbered Years

Visiting Log   ☐S ☐M ☐T ☐W ☐T ☐S ☐F   Date:

Child		Location	
Cutodial Parcent		Non-Custodial Parcent	
Style of Visit			
Expected Start Time		Actual Start Time	
Expected End Time		Actual End Time	

Phone Calls Log

Initiated by		With whom	
Time		Length of call	

Notes: _____

Child Name:		Paying Parcent		Date:	

Payment Information

Date Due	Expected Amount	Actual Amount	Date Paid	Balance

Agreement References

Agreement	Document	Page	Note

Holiday Schedule

Holiday	Time	Even-Numbered Years	Odd-Numbered Years

Visiting Log   S M T W T S F   Date:

Child		Location	
Cutodial Parcent		Non-Custodial Parcent	
Style of Visit			
Expected Start Time		Actual Start Time	
Expected End Time		Actual End Time	

Phone Calls Log

Initiated by		With whom	
Time		Length of call	

Notes: _____

_____

_____

Child Name:		Paying Parcent		Date:	

Payment Information

Date Due	Expected Amount	Actual Amount	Date Paid	Balance

Agreement References

Agreement	Document	Page	Note

Holiday Schedule

Holiday	Time	Even-Numbered Years	Odd-Numbered Years

Visiting Log S M T W T S F   Date:

Child		Location	
Cutodial Parcent		Non-Custodial Parcent	
Style of Visit			
Expected Start Time		Actual Start Time	
Expected End Time		Actual End Time	

Phone Calls Log

Initiated by		With whom	
Time		Length of call	

Notes: _____

_____

Child Name:		Paying Parcent		Date:	

Payment Information

Date Due	Expected Amount	Actual Amount	Date Paid	Balance

Agreement References

Agreement	Document	Page	Note

Holiday Schedule

Holiday	Time	Even-Numbered Years	Odd-Numbered Years

Visiting Log   S M T W T S F   Date:

Child		Location	
Cutodial Parcent		Non-Custodial Parcent	
Style of Visit			
Expected Start Time		Actual Start Time	
Expected End Time		Actual End Time	

Phone Calls Log

Initiated by		With whom	
Time		Length of call	

Notes: _____

_____

_____

Child Name:		Paying Parcent		Date:	

Payment Information

Date Due	Expected Amount	Actual Amount	Date Paid	Balance

Agreement References

Agreement	Document	Page	Note

Holiday Schedule

Holiday	Time	Even-Numbered Years	Odd-Numbered Years

Visiting Log

☐ S ☐ M ☐ T ☐ W ☐ T ☐ S ☐ F   Date:

Child		Location	
Cutodial Parcent		Non-Custodial Parcent	
Style of Visit			
Expected Start Time		Actual Start Time	
Expected End Time		Actual End Time	

Phone Calls Log

Initiated by		With whom	
Time		Length of call	

Notes: _____

Child Name:		Paying Parcent		Date:	

Payment Information

Date Due	Expected Amount	Actual Amount	Date Paid	Balance

Agreement References

Agreement	Document	Page	Note

Holiday Schedule

Holiday	Time	Even-Numbered Years	Odd-Numbered Years

Visiting Log   S M T W T S F   Date:

Child		Location	
Cutodial Parcent		Non-Custodial Parcent	
Style of Visit			
Expected Start Time		Actual Start Time	
Expected End Time		Actual End Time	

Phone Calls Log

Initiated by		With whom	
Time		Length of call	

Notes: _____

_____

_____

Child Name:		Paying Parcent		Date:	

Payment Information

Date Due	Expected Amount	Actual Amount	Date Paid	Balance

Agreement References

Agreement	Document	Page	Note

Holiday Schedule

Holiday	Time	Even-Numbered Years	Odd-Numbered Years

Visiting Log   ☐S ☐M ☐T ☐W ☐T ☐S ☐F   Date:

Child		Location	
Cutodial Parcent		Non-Custodial Parcent	
Style of Visit			
Expected Start Time		Actual Start Time	
Expected End Time		Actual End Time	

Phone Calls Log

Initiated by		With whom	
Time		Length of call	

Notes: _____
_____
_____

Child Name:		Paying Parcent		Date:	

Payment Information

Date Due	Expected Amount	Actual Amount	Date Paid	Balance

Agreement References

Agreement	Document	Page	Note

Holiday Schedule

Holiday	Time	Even-Numbered Years	Odd-Numbered Years

Visiting Log   S M T W T S F   Date:

Child		Location	
Cutodial Parcent		Non-Custodial Parcent	
Style of Visit			
Expected Start Time		Actual Start Time	
Expected End Time		Actual End Time	

Phone Calls Log

Initiated by		With whom	
Time		Length of call	

Notes: _____

_____

_____

Child Name:		Paying Parcent		Date:	

Payment Information

Date Due	Expected Amount	Actual Amount	Date Paid	Balance

Agreement References

Agreement	Document	Page	Note

Holiday Schedule

Holiday	Time	Even-Numbered Years	Odd-Numbered Years

Visiting Log ☐S ☐M ☐T ☐W ☐T ☐S ☐F   Date:

Child		Location	
Cutodial Parcent		Non-Custodial Parcent	
Style of Visit			
Expected Start Time		Actual Start Time	
Expected End Time		Actual End Time	

Phone Calls Log

Initiated by		With whom	
Time		Length of call	

Notes: _____

| Child Name: | | | Paying Parcent | | Date: | |

Payment Information

Date Due	Expected Amount	Actual Amount	Date Paid	Balance

Agreement References

Agreement	Document	Page	Note

Holiday Schedule

Holiday	Time	Even-Numbered Years	Odd-Numbered Years

Visiting Log   S M T W T S F   Date:

Child		Location	
Cutodial Parcent		Non-Custodial Parcent	
Style of Visit			
Expected Start Time		Actual Start Time	
Expected End Time		Actual End Time	

Phone Calls Log

Initiated by		With whom	
Time		Length of call	

Notes: _____

_____

_____

| Child Name: | | Paying Parcent | | Date: | |

Payment Information

Date Due	Expected Amount	Actual Amount	Date Paid	Balance

Agreement References

Agreement	Document	Page	Note

Holiday Schedule

Holiday	Time	Even-Numbered Years	Odd-Numbered Years

Visiting Log   S M T W T S F   Date:

Child		Location	
Cutodial Parcent		Non-Custodial Parcent	
Style of Visit			
Expected Start Time		Actual Start Time	
Expected End Time		Actual End Time	

Phone Calls Log

Initiated by		With whom	
Time		Length of call	

Notes: _____
_____

Child Name:		Paying Parcent		Date:	

Payment Information

Date Due	Expected Amount	Actual Amount	Date Paid	Balance

Agreement References

Agreement	Document	Page	Note

Holiday Schedule

Holiday	Time	Even-Numbered Years	Odd-Numbered Years

Visiting Log   S M T W T S F   Date:

Child		Location	
Cutodial Parcent		Non-Custodial Parcent	
Style of Visit			
Expected Start Time		Actual Start Time	
Expected End Time		Actual End Time	

Phone Calls Log

Initiated by		With whom	
Time		Length of call	

Notes: _____

_____

_____

Child Name:		Paying Parcent		Date:	

Payment Information

Date Due	Expected Amount	Actual Amount	Date Paid	Balance

Agreement References

Agreement	Document	Page	Note

Holiday Schedule

Holiday	Time	Even-Numbered Years	Odd-Numbered Years

Visiting Log   S M T W T S F   Date:

Child		Location	
Cutodial Parcent		Non-Custodial Parcent	
Style of Visit			
Expected Start Time		Actual Start Time	
Expected End Time		Actual End Time	

Phone Calls Log

Initiated by		With whom	
Time		Length of call	

Notes: _____

_____

_____

| Child Name: | | Paying Parent | | Date: | |

Payment Information

Date Due	Expected Amount	Actual Amount	Date Paid	Balance

Agreement References

Agreement	Document	Page	Note

Holiday Schedule

Holiday	Time	Even-Numbered Years	Odd-Numbered Years

Visiting Log ☐S ☐M ☐T ☐W ☐T ☐S ☐F   Date:

Child		Location	
Cutodial Parcent		Non-Custodial Parcent	
Style of Visit			
Expected Start Time		Actual Start Time	
Expected End Time		Actual End Time	

Phone Calls Log

Initiated by		With whom	
Time		Length of call	

Notes: _____

_____

_____

Child Name:		Paying Parcent		Date:	

Payment Information

Date Due	Expected Amount	Actual Amount	Date Paid	Balance

Agreement References

Agreement	Document	Page	Note

Holiday Schedule

Holiday	Time	Even-Numbered Years	Odd-Numbered Years

Visiting Log   ☐S ☐M ☐T ☐W ☐T ☐S ☐F   Date: _____

Child		Location	
Cutodial Parcent		Non-Custodial Parcent	
Style of Visit			
Expected Start Time		Actual Start Time	
Expected End Time		Actual End Time	

Phone Calls Log

Initiated by		With whom	
Time		Length of call	

Notes: _____

_____

_____

Child Name:		Paying Parcent		Date:	

Payment Information

Date Due	Expected Amount	Actual Amount	Date Paid	Balance

Agreement References

Agreement	Document	Page	Note

Holiday Schedule

Holiday	Time	Even-Numbered Years	Odd-Numbered Years

Visiting Log   [S] [M] [T] [W] [T] [S] [F]   Date:

Child		Location	
Cutodial Parcent		Non-Custodial Parcent	
Style of Visit			
Expected Start Time		Actual Start Time	
Expected End Time		Actual End Time	

Phone Calls Log

Initiated by		With whom	
Time		Length of call	

Notes: _____

_____

_____

| Child Name: | | Paying Parcent | | Date: | |

Payment Information

Date Due	Expected Amount	Actual Amount	Date Paid	Balance

Agreement References

Agreement	Document	Page	Note

Holiday Schedule

Holiday	Time	Even-Numbered Years	Odd-Numbered Years

Visiting Log   [S] [M] [T] [W] [T] [S] [F]   Date:

Child		Location	
Cutodial Parcent		Non-Custodial Parcent	
Style of Visit			
Expected Start Time		Actual Start Time	
Expected End Time		Actual End Time	

Phone Calls Log

Initiated by		With whom	
Time		Length of call	

Notes: _____
_____
_____

Child Name:		Paying Parcent		Date:	

Payment Information

Date Due	Expected Amount	Actual Amount	Date Paid	Balance

Agreement References

Agreement	Document	Page	Note

Holiday Schedule

Holiday	Time	Even-Numbered Years	Odd-Numbered Years

Visiting Log   S M T W T S F   Date:

Child		Location	
Cutodial Parcent		Non-Custodial Parcent	
Style of Visit			
Expected Start Time		Actual Start Time	
Expected End Time		Actual End Time	

Phone Calls Log

Initiated by		With whom	
Time		Length of call	

Notes: _____

_____

_____

| Child Name: | | Paying Parcent | | Date: | |

Payment Information

Date Due	Expected Amount	Actual Amount	Date Paid	Balance

Agreement References

Agreement	Document	Page	Note

Holiday Schedule

Holiday	Time	Even-Numbered Years	Odd-Numbered Years

Visiting Log   S M T W T S F   Date:

Child		Location	
Cutodial Parcent		Non-Custodial Parcent	
Style of Visit			
Expected Start Time		Actual Start Time	
Expected End Time		Actual End Time	

Phone Calls Log

Initiated by		With whom	
Time		Length of call	

Notes: _____

_____

_____

| Child Name: | | Paying Parcent | | Date: | |

Payment Information

Date Due	Expected Amount	Actual Amount	Date Paid	Balance

Agreement References

Agreement	Document	Page	Note

Holiday Schedule

Holiday	Time	Even-Numbered Years	Odd-Numbered Years

Visiting Log   S M T W T S F   Date:

Child		Location	
Cutodial Parcent		Non-Custodial Parcent	
Style of Visit			
Expected Start Time		Actual Start Time	
Expected End Time		Actual End Time	

Phone Calls Log

Initiated by		With whom	
Time		Length of call	

Notes: _____

_____

_____

| Child Name: | | Paying Parcent | | Date: | |

Payment Information

Date Due	Expected Amount	Actual Amount	Date Paid	Balance

Agreement References

Agreement	Document	Page	Note

Holiday Schedule

Holiday	Time	Even-Numbered Years	Odd-Numbered Years

Visiting Log   S M T W T S F   Date:

Child		Location	
Cutodial Parcent		Non-Custodial Parcent	
Style of Visit			
Expected Start Time		Actual Start Time	
Expected End Time		Actual End Time	

Phone Calls Log

Initiated by		With whom	
Time		Length of call	

Notes: _____

_____

_____

Child Name:		Paying Parent		Date:	

Payment Information

Date Due	Expected Amount	Actual Amount	Date Paid	Balance

Agreement References

Agreement	Document	Page	Note

Holiday Schedule

Holiday	Time	Even-Numbered Years	Odd-Numbered Years

Visiting Log S M T W T S F   Date:

Child		Location	
Cutodial Parcent		Non-Custodial Parcent	
Style of Visit			
Expected Start Time		Actual Start Time	
Expected End Time		Actual End Time	

Phone Calls Log

Initiated by		With whom	
Time		Length of call	

Notes: _____

_____

_____

Child Name:		Paying Parcent		Date:	

Payment Information

Date Due	Expected Amount	Actual Amount	Date Paid	Balance

Agreement References

Agreement	Document	Page	Note

Holiday Schedule

Holiday	Time	Even-Numbered Years	Odd-Numbered Years

Visiting Log ☐S ☐M ☐T ☐W ☐T ☐S ☐F   Date:

Child		Location	
Cutodial Parcent		Non-Custodial Parcent	
Style of Visit			
Expected Start Time		Actual Start Time	
Expected End Time		Actual End Time	

Phone Calls Log

Initiated by		With whom	
Time		Length of call	

Notes: _____

Child Name:		Paying Parcent		Date:	

Payment Information

Date Due	Expected Amount	Actual Amount	Date Paid	Balance

Agreement References

Agreement	Document	Page	Note

Holiday Schedule

Holiday	Time	Even-Numbered Years	Odd-Numbered Years

Visiting Log   S M T W T S F   Date:

Child		Location	
Cutodial Parcent		Non-Custodial Parcent	
Style of Visit			
Expected Start Time		Actual Start Time	
Expected End Time		Actual End Time	

Phone Calls Log

Initiated by		With whom	
Time		Length of call	

Notes: _____

_____

_____

Child Name:		Paying Parcent		Date:	

Payment Information

Date Due	Expected Amount	Actual Amount	Date Paid	Balance

Agreement References

Agreement	Document	Page	Note

Holiday Schedule

Holiday	Time	Even-Numbered Years	Odd-Numbered Years

Visiting Log S M T W T S F   Date:

Child		Location	
Cutodial Parcent		Non-Custodial Parcent	
Style of Visit			
Expected Start Time		Actual Start Time	
Expected End Time		Actual End Time	

Phone Calls Log

Initiated by		With whom	
Time		Length of call	

Notes: _____

_____

_____

Child Name:		Paying Parent		Date:	

Payment Information

Date Due	Expected Amount	Actual Amount	Date Paid	Balance

Agreement References

Agreement	Document	Page	Note

Holiday Schedule

Holiday	Time	Even-Numbered Years	Odd-Numbered Years

Visiting Log   S M T W T S F   Date:

Child		Location	
Cutodial Parcent		Non-Custodial Parcent	
Style of Visit			
Expected Start Time		Actual Start Time	
Expected End Time		Actual End Time	

Phone Calls Log

Initiated by		With whom	
Time		Length of call	

Notes: _____

_____

_____

Child Name:		Paying Parcent		Date:	

Payment Information

Date Due	Expected Amount	Actual Amount	Date Paid	Balance

Agreement References

Agreement	Document	Page	Note

Holiday Schedule

Holiday	Time	Even-Numbered Years	Odd-Numbered Years

Visiting Log   S M T W T S F   Date:

Child		Location	
Cutodial Parcent		Non-Custodial Parcent	
Style of Visit			
Expected Start Time		Actual Start Time	
Expected End Time		Actual End Time	

Phone Calls Log

Initiated by		With whom	
Time		Length of call	

Notes: _____

Child Name:		Paying Parcent		Date:	

Payment Information

Date Due	Expected Amount	Actual Amount	Date Paid	Balance

Agreement References

Agreement	Document	Page	Note

Holiday Schedule

Holiday	Time	Even-Numbered Years	Odd-Numbered Years

Visiting Log ☐S ☐M ☐T ☐W ☐T ☐S ☐F   Date:

Child		Location	
Cutodial Parcent		Non-Custodial Parcent	
Style of Visit			
Expected Start Time		Actual Start Time	
Expected End Time		Actual End Time	

Phone Calls Log

Initiated by		With whom	
Time		Length of call	

Notes: _____

_____

_____

| Child Name: | | Paying Parcent | | Date: | |

Payment Information

Date Due	Expected Amount	Actual Amount	Date Paid	Balance

Agreement References

Agreement	Document	Page	Note

Holiday Schedule

Holiday	Time	Even-Numbered Years	Odd-Numbered Years

Visiting Log   ☐S ☐M ☐T ☐W ☐T ☐S ☐F   Date:

Child		Location	
Cutodial Parcent		Non-Custodial Parcent	
Style of Visit			
Expected Start Time		Actual Start Time	
Expected End Time		Actual End Time	

Phone Calls Log

Initiated by		With whom	
Time		Length of call	

Notes: _____

_____

Child Name:			Paying Parcent		Date:	

Payment Information

Date Due	Expected Amount	Actual Amount	Date Paid	Balance

Agreement References

Agreement	Document	Page	Note

Holiday Schedule

Holiday	Time	Even-Numbered Years	Odd-Numbered Years

Visiting Log [S] [M] [T] [W] [T] [S] [F]   Date:

Child		Location	
Cutodial Parcent		Non-Custodial Parcent	
Style of Visit			
Expected Start Time		Actual Start Time	
Expected End Time		Actual End Time	

Phone Calls Log

Initiated by		With whom	
Time		Length of call	

Notes: _____

_____

_____

Child Name:		Paying Parcent		Date:	

Payment Information

Date Due	Expected Amount	Actual Amount	Date Paid	Balance

Agreement References

Agreement	Document	Page	Note

Holiday Schedule

Holiday	Time	Even-Numbered Years	Odd-Numbered Years

Visiting Log   [S] [M] [T] [W] [T] [S] [F]   Date:

Child		Location	
Cutodial Parcent		Non-Custodial Parcent	
Style of Visit			
Expected Start Time		Actual Start Time	
Expected End Time		Actual End Time	

Phone Calls Log

Initiated by		With whom	
Time		Length of call	

Notes: _____

Child Name:		Paying Parcent		Date:	

Payment Information

Date Due	Expected Amount	Actual Amount	Date Paid	Balance

Agreement References

Agreement	Document	Page	Note

Holiday Schedule

Holiday	Time	Even-Numbered Years	Odd-Numbered Years

Visiting Log   S M T W T S F   Date:

Child		Location	
Cutodial Parcent		Non-Custodial Parcent	
Style of Visit			
Expected Start Time		Actual Start Time	
Expected End Time		Actual End Time	

Phone Calls Log

Initiated by		With whom	
Time		Length of call	

Notes: _____

_____

_____

| Child Name: | | Paying Parcent | | Date: | |

Payment Information

Date Due	Expected Amount	Actual Amount	Date Paid	Balance

Agreement References

Agreement	Document	Page	Note

Holiday Schedule

Holiday	Time	Even-Numbered Years	Odd-Numbered Years

Visiting Log   ☐S ☐M ☐T ☐W ☐T ☐S ☐F   Date: _____

Child		Location	
Cutodial Parcent		Non-Custodial Parcent	
Style of Visit			
Expected Start Time		Actual Start Time	
Expected End Time		Actual End Time	

Phone Calls Log

Initiated by		With whom	
Time		Length of call	

Notes: _____

_____

| Child Name: | | Paying Parcent | | Date: | |

Payment Information

Date Due	Expected Amount	Actual Amount	Date Paid	Balance

Agreement References

Agreement	Document	Page	Note

Holiday Schedule

Holiday	Time	Even-Numbered Years	Odd-Numbered Years

Visiting Log [S] [M] [T] [W] [T] [S] [F] Date:

Child		Location	
Cutodial Parcent		Non-Custodial Parcent	
Style of Visit			
Expected Start Time		Actual Start Time	
Expected End Time		Actual End Time	

Phone Calls Log

Initiated by		With whom	
Time		Length of call	

Notes: _____

_____

_____

Child Name:		Paying Parcent		Date:	

Payment Information

Date Due	Expected Amount	Actual Amount	Date Paid	Balance

Agreement References

Agreement	Document	Page	Note

Holiday Schedule

Holiday	Time	Even-Numbered Years	Odd-Numbered Years

Visiting Log   [S] [M] [T] [W] [T] [S] [F]   Date:

Child		Location	
Cutodial Parcent		Non-Custodial Parcent	
Style of Visit			
Expected Start Time		Actual Start Time	
Expected End Time		Actual End Time	

Phone Calls Log

Initiated by		With whom	
Time		Length of call	

Notes: _____

Child Name:		Paying Parcent		Date:	

Payment Information

Date Due	Expected Amount	Actual Amount	Date Paid	Balance

Agreement References

Agreement	Document	Page	Note

Holiday Schedule

Holiday	Time	Even-Numbered Years	Odd-Numbered Years

Visiting Log   S M T W T S F   Date:

Child		Location	
Cutodial Parcent		Non-Custodial Parcent	
Style of Visit			
Expected Start Time		Actual Start Time	
Expected End Time		Actual End Time	

Phone Calls Log

Initiated by		With whom	
Time		Length of call	

Notes: _____

_____

_____

Child Name:		Paying Parcent		Date:	

Payment Information

Date Due	Expected Amount	Actual Amount	Date Paid	Balance

Agreement References

Agreement	Document	Page	Note

Holiday Schedule

Holiday	Time	Even-Numbered Years	Odd-Numbered Years

Visiting Log   S M T W T S F   Date:

Child		Location	
Cutodial Parcent		Non-Custodial Parcent	
Style of Visit			
Expected Start Time		Actual Start Time	
Expected End Time		Actual End Time	

Phone Calls Log

Initiated by		With whom	
Time		Length of call	

Notes: _____

Made in the USA
Las Vegas, NV
23 March 2025